A Beginner's Guide to

AUTISM
SPECTRUM
DISORDERS

of related interest

My Child Has Autism, Now What?
10 Steps to Get You Started
Susan Larson Kidd
ISBN 978 1 84905 841 4

Asperger Syndrome – What Teachers Need to Know
Second Edition
Matt Winter
With Clare Lawrence
ISBN 978 1 84905 203 0

The ASD Workbook
Understanding Your Autism Spectrum Disorder
Penny Kershaw
ISBN 978 1 84905 195 8

Hints and Tips for Helping Children with Autism Spectrum Disorders
Useful Strategies for Home, School, and the Community
Dion E. Betts and Nancy J. Patrick
ISBN 978 1 84310 896 2

A Beginner's Guide to

AUTISM
SPECTRUM
DISORDERS

Essential Information for
Parents and Professionals

Paul G. Taylor

Jessica Kingsley *Publishers*
London and Philadelphia

First published in 2011
by Jessica Kingsley Publishers
116 Pentonville Road
London N1 9JB, UK
and
400 Market Street, Suite 400
Philadelphia, PA 19106, USA

www.jkp.com

Library of Congress Cataloging in Publication Data
Taylor, Paul G. (Paul Gordon), 1945-
    A beginner's guide to autism spectrum disorders : essential
information for parents and professionals / Paul G. Taylor.
       p. cm.
    Includes index.
    ISBN 978-1-84905-233-7 (alk. paper)
    1. Autism spectrum disorders. I. Title.
    RC553.A88T39 2011
    616.85'882--dc22

                                        2011001880

British Library Cataloguing in Publication Data
A CIP catalogue record for this book is available from the British Library

ISBN 978 1 84905 233 7

Printed and bound in Great Britain

To Frances

Contents

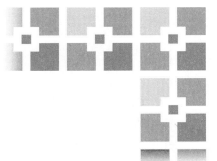

Acknowledgements

I am a consultant paediatrician working in a regional general hospital in New Zealand.

This book acknowledges the many children, young persons and adults, and their families, who have allowed me to work with them to confirm a diagnosis of autism spectrum disorder (ASD). Just about all of them have allowed me to continue to work with them to confront the challenges that face them in dealing with all that the world throws at them because of their differences.

What follows is a mix of what I have learnt from every family I have worked with and from each of the many fellow professionals who have shared their knowledge and wisdom with me. All this has shaped my own thinking into how to provide the best understanding and support I can to each individual, each family, each teacher, each school and each workplace facing the challenge of adapting to someone with ASD.

Over the past 12 years I have enjoyed taking the message of ASD to families, schools and fellow professionals in the form of talks, which have constantly evolved into what is now the substance of this book. Thanks to all those who have sat through my ramblings and asked the pointed questions that improved my thinking.

My thanks to Angie and Pip (they know who they are) who field tested the original manuscript, to Lisa Hadfield who provided the snippet on p.62 and to Lesley Smith who edited the first draft.

My wife, Frances, went over the final draft with a fine-tooth comb and made many useful suggestions which clarified my writing. As always I am grateful for her wisdom and encouragement.

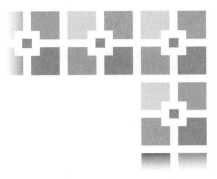

Introduction

Thank you for picking up this book. I'm hoping you won't put it down until you get to the end. That's one reason why I have tried to keep it short. The other reason is that there are lots of good, clever and comprehensive books out there so there is really no need for another long academic tome.

I have been around for a long time and spent many years helping parents, extended family members, teachers, school boards, fellow professionals and, increasingly, adults come to grips with a diagnosis of autism spectrum disorder (ASD).

Each time I make this diagnosis I am asked for a source of further information to explain what is going on. At this point in the proceedings I always find myself at a bit of a loss.

The experience I have accumulated and the comments I have received from all these people have given me the confidence to think it might be helpful for others if I were to share my learning and my thinking about ASD with those who are confronting the diagnosis of ASD for the first time. So I threw caution to the wind and decided to write this book.

ASD is a diagnosis which demands a total redesign of conventional thinking in order to understand what goes on in the mind of a person who has this condition.

I believe that the framework I have developed over the course of giving many talks on this subject will help those who are coming across the diagnosis for the first time to get their heads around the basic concepts which must be understood before we can begin to create the kind of world in which the children, young people and adults we aim to help can survive, grow and prosper.

I hope you can cope with the style of this book. Mostly I write from the perspective of someone trying to get a message across, adult to adult. At other times I will slip into the persona of someone with ASD who is describing things from his or her perspective. This is not accidental. I would like you, the reader, to be able to develop the knack of flipping from your own objective and subjective world into the world as seen by someone who has ASD.

As you will learn, this knack of walking in the same shoes as somebody who has ASD is essential if you are to make progress in living and working with him.

At times I overstate a point I am trying to make. In the real world things are not always as black and white as I sometimes make out. I use exaggeration not because I don't have a sense of perspective but because there are some points I feel strongly about. In a short book like this there is not enough space to dissect a problem meticulously and provide a detailed and balanced dissertation. If you are looking for something like that, there are some really good books available that go into far more detail than this one does.

But I do believe this book is a good starting point.

Part I

ASD – The Simple Facts

1

Nuts and Bolts

Autism
Autistic Spectrum Disorder
Borderline Autism
Autism Spectrum Disorder
Pervasive Developmental Disorder Not Otherwise
Specified
High-functioning Autism
Asperger's
PDD-NOS
Autistic
Asperger Syndrome
Pervasive Developmental Disorder
PDD
Aspie
ASD
Autistic Tendencies

These are some of the terms you might hear used to describe the kind of person this book is about. They are often used indiscriminately and interchangeably.

Many of these terms may be used to describe the same child. This can create confusion, undermine confidence in the diagnosis, get in the way of good communication and make effective planning more difficult.

This confusion arises because of a lack of agreement across the world on what name or names to use. The World Health Organization has tried over the years to come up with a system of classification to help us get to a common agreement on the correct name to call just about any medical condition. This is called the International Classification of Diseases (ICD), which is now in its tenth version called, not unsurprisingly, the ICD-10.

The American Psychiatric Association has been doing the same thing for conditions which affect how the brain thinks. Their classification system is published in the *Diagnostic and Statistical Manual of* (DSM) which is currently in its fourth edition and is called the DSM-IV.

The DSM-IV has a group of conditions it calls the pervasive developmental disorders (PDD). This group includes

- autistic disorder [more commonly referred to as autism spectrum disorder/ASD]

- Asperger's disorder [more commonly referred to as Asperger syndrome/AS]

- pervasive developmental disorder not otherwise specified (PDD-NOS).

There are also two other very rare disorders we don't need to worry about in this book (these are Rett's disorder and childhood disintegrative disorder, just so you know). Just where any one of the three main disorders begins or ends can be a matter of personal judgement and preference. This is where confusion can arise, because one person's AS can be someone else's PDD-NOS.

Most people have given up on this and now call everything in this group autism, or autism spectrum disorder or autistic spectrum disorder. For these people the DSM-IV has become an irrelevance.

The American Psychiatric Association has signalled that in the next edition of the DSM they will do away with the three major subgroups (ASD, AS and PDD-NOS). They are proposing that everything will be called autism spectrum disorder. In addition, the things that are necessary for the diagnosis may be simplified. This is not yet set in stone and many people are challenging this new proposal, especially some vocal adults who are proud of their diagnosis of Asperger syndrome.

However, this new approach as to how to call a spade a spade is becoming firmly entrenched across the world, so for this book I have chosen to go with the flow and call everything autism spectrum disorder (ASD).

We will nevertheless still use the current three DSM-IV standards for diagnosis because these really do help the understanding about what is special in people who have ASD. If you or the person who is the reason you are reading this book has been diagnosed with any of the terms at the beginning of this chapter, then this book is specifically aimed to help you. The term autism spectrum disorder sits perfectly with any of the other terms and sooner or later everything will fall into line.

2

Diagnosis

The autism spectrum disorders

In this group of disorders, which are the focus of this book, the DSM-IV specifies impairments in three specific areas of behaviour which have to be present in order to make a diagnosis. These three areas are:

Impairment of social interaction

- Difficulty in understanding the non-verbal aspects of social interaction, such as being able to understand facial expressions, turn taking in conversation and understanding what is going on in the other person's mind.

- Difficulty in making friends and interacting with people of the same age and preferring to associate with younger or older people.

- Not seeking to share experiences, objects, activities or space.

- Difficulty in sharing social and emotional interactions with other people.

Impairment of communication

- Absence or significant restriction of spoken language.

- Difficulty in engaging in conversation with other people by listening to and responding to what the other person is saying.

- Using stereotyped/repetitive/idiosyncratic language.

- Having no interest in participating in spontaneous make-believe play with other people of the same age.

Impairment of activity and interests

- Encompassing and restricting preoccupation with a small range of ideas or things or topics.

- Obsession with ritual, order and repetitive behaviours.

- Showing repetitive motor mannerisms such as hand flapping, singing or making particular noises.

- Preoccupation with parts of objects which interferes with understanding how the whole object works.

According to the latest research, published in 2010, about one person in every hundred people may have autism spectrum disorder (ASD). We are talking about a sizeable segment of the population here. In order to ensure that as parents and professionals we do the best we can in working with someone who has ASD, many of us are going to have to do a whole lot of learning. You will find that this effort pays off when you see the difference you can make for the person who needs our understanding.

Fine wine

In some respects ASD is like fine wine.

Let's try to classify wine. We might say there are three broad types of wine – white, red and rosé.

Within each of these three broad groups there may be many different grape varieties, such as chardonnay, sauvignon blanc, riesling, pinot gris, cabernet sauvignon, zinfandel, pinot noir, and so on.

Or perhaps we can divide wine by region of origin starting with the country, then region, then the town or village and then the specific vineyard and even the specific row of plants.

Then there is vintage – wine from one year in the same block of the same vineyard might be quite different from the previous or the following year.

Then there is the style of wine the winemaker tries to achieve using his experience and his art.

Then there is the effect of cellaring and handling of the wine on the development of its character.

And finally there is the context in which the wine is consumed – temperature, accompanying food, and so on.

So wine can be anything from a generic type of grape beverage to something unique, specific and unreproducible.

And so it is with ASD. We may generalize on many features which are shared by people with ASD but in reality there are no two people with ASD who are the same or who share exactly the same presentation.

So if you know somebody with ASD you will not find a complete and accurate description of him in this book, or anywhere else for that matter. The best you can hope for is a series of general statements which may or may not be relevant to the person you have in mind. Exceptions to the rule are frequent and do not necessarily invalidate the diagnosis.

3

Autism Spectrum Disorders are Hard-wired

Now we are beginning to get down to the nitty gritty of ASD.

Nobody has as yet discovered precisely what causes ASD. There have been many theories proposed over the years but none has ever been proved or really gained acceptance. Some theories have led parents to spend vast amounts of emotional energy and money in the understandable hope that something miraculous might be achieved for their affected child.

ASDs tend to run in families. The pattern of occurrence within families is unpredictable, varied and patchy, which suggests that ASD is not a disorder caused by a single gene. The way in which ASD presents itself is so varied as to strongly suggest that there are several genes involved. Furthermore it is possible that something in the very early developmental stages of somebody with ASD may 'switch on' a gene or series of genes which then leads to ASD emerging. We are probably looking at a large number of distinct genetic situations which just happen to have the same main features. So we lump them together under the same name.

In practice this is OK. The general assumptions we make about ASD tend to lead to interventions that work in most situations.

To recap the previous chapter, ASD is a hard-wired difference in thinking patterns that some people are born with. As we have seen, in ASD there are differences in communication, differences in social interaction, and differences in range and intensity of interests. The degree of difference varies from severe at one end to mild and subtle at the other. In the old classification, severe ASD was and still is called autistic spectrum disorder (ASD). A milder form of ASD results in a specific pattern of differences often known as Asperger syndrome (AS). Other people with ASD fit into the mild end of the range of differences, which used to be called pervasive developmental disorder not otherwise specified, usually abbreviated to PDD-NOS.

Children, young people and adults with ASD can be endlessly fascinating. They can also be endlessly challenging. Their behaviour can be very hard to understand and to cope with. Using conventional ways of trying to understand and control behaviour is usually unsuccessful and frustrating.

Why is this?

Apple computers run OS and PCs run Windows

Imagine that instead of being human beings we were all computers. I would guess that most of you would immediately think of yourself as a typical personal computer running Microsoft Windows. Some of you might choose to be an Apple computer. Most personal computers in the world are based on Windows operating systems, while a small percentage are based on Apple OS operating systems.

Those of you who choose to be a Windows-based computer can run any program designed for the Windows operating system. You can take a program from one Windows computer and run it on another Windows computer without any problem. All you Windows computers share the same operating system and you all 'think' in the same way. You can communicate with each other because you are designed to 'think' in the same way.

Those of you who choose to use Apple OS are in the same situation as far as running and communicating with each other goes. Any program designed to run on Apple OS will run on any Apple computer. You Apple computers can communicate and share with each other because you are also designed to 'think' the same way.

There is only one problem – if you are a Windows computer you cannot understand Apple programs and if you are an Apple computer you cannot understand Windows programs. Apple computers are 'hard-wired' differently to Windows computers.

Now think of ASD as being a hard-wired difference in how brain circuits are organized. Think of people with ASD as being Apple computers trying to exist in a world of Windows-based PC computers. Both Apple computers and Windows computers are very good at doing what they were built for. They just go about it differently.

If you try to run programs written for Windows computers on Apple computers nothing happens. The screen stays blank or an error message pops up. Or perhaps the Apple computer will crash. It doesn't matter how often you try to run the Windows program on the Apple computer, you will never get it to work.

However, if you run programs written for Apple OS on the Apple computer you will get wonderful and reliable results.

And of course you can turn this example around to a Windows point of view in which you find that the PC will not understand or run programs written for Apple OS. It's an incompatibility that runs in both directions.

We tend to prefer Windows-based computers for things like word processing and spreadsheets. Apple computers are often chosen because they are really good at doing music and graphics.

So getting back to humans, think of the situation as most people being Windows-based. We understand each other because we run the same operating system. We take much for granted about how and what other people think and we are usually about right much of the time. We use words like insight, intuition and empathy when we describe the beliefs we have about what makes other people tick. Because we are 'Windows-based' we find it hard to communicate with someone with ASD who is 'Apple-based'. We tend to make assumptions based on our Windows thinking and our Windows experience and then get frustrated when the Apple-based person with ASD does not respond the way we expect.

There is, of course, nothing wrong with Apple computers. It's just that they don't 'do' Windows. They 'do' Apple!

You cannot change the underlying brain operating system of someone with ASD, or someone who does not have ASD. The majority of us are often called 'neuro-typical' by people who have ASD; in other words many people with ASD have come to understand that there is a difference in thinking mechanisms, styles and patterns between them and what the rest of us might call 'normal' people.

Disorder or difference?

It is important to look at the language here. The DSM-IV talks of 'disorders'. We talk of 'normal'. This type of language tends to encourage the notion that there is something 'wrong' if you have ASD. This is a value-laden concept, because you can only be 'wrong' if you are not 'right'.

I would argue that it is disrespectful and unhelpful to use terms that convey this kind of value-laden undertone when we talk about people with ASD. In my view there is nothing at all 'wrong'. What we see are 'differences', some of which may lead to 'impairments'.

These 'impairments' only exist in the eyes of the observer, be she a mother, a sister or a classroom teacher. The people with the 'impairment' do not need to feel impaired. Why should they? Left to their own devices their brains tell them what to do that suits their preferences. Problems only arise when we impose our 'normal' pattern of thinking and expectations on them. This meets our needs but ignores what the person with ASD sees as his needs.

With 'neuro-typical' behaviour we resolve conflict over time by the use of rules, social norms, values, and the development of the ability to negotiate and compromise based on an understanding of what might be going on in the other person's mind and what might be motivating her.

The person with ASD does not do 'negotiation' or 'compromise'. Nor for that matter does he do a lot of other sophisticated things which are part and parcel of getting along in a group, be it a family, a school class, a school playground or a workplace. This is not necessarily because he doesn't want to be part of a group, have friends and enjoy relationships. The barrier is that he doesn't know how to act within the social norms of his age peers. He does not 'get it' and, over time, his group leaves him out.

Where is this leading us?

The point of understanding some fixed truths about people with ASD is that you are going to have to make some changes in how you approach your interactions with them. You are going to have to abandon the conventional notions you have about behaviour, development, and learning and teaching which you have carefully nurtured over your lifetime experience as a member of our 'neuro-typical' society. What you have learnt, what you have become very good at using in your contacts with other people is useless when you have to deal with someone with ASD.

Get used to it. If you do, you will make the world of difference to the person with ASD and the world of difference to yourself. You will all begin to make progress, avoid the traps that have entangled you so far, and begin to create a new paradigm for success.

So, where do we begin?

4

How to Recognize the Person Who Has ASD

This is not rocket science.

Let's start by revisiting the three core differences (impairments) which are at the heart of ASD. These are impairments in:

- communication

- social interaction

- range or intensity of interests.

In addition we will often see a range of sensory intolerances, possibly some unusual physical movement mannerisms and, as you will come to understand, behaviour that indicates underlying anxiety.

Let's see what features of behaviour these impairments produce.

When they are free to play with other children, such as at school break time, children with ASD avoid social contact with other children. For example, they may find a secluded place on the edge of the playground or ask to go to the library. At home they rarely ask for other children to come round to play, although there may be one or two children they feel comfortable with for a short time. However, chances are that although they accept the other child being there they will not engage in reciprocal play. They prefer to play by themselves alongside their guest. They are usually not invited over by other children. They are regarded as being a bit strange, and others feel awkward in their company. This does not seem to be a problem to the child with ASD, although many such children tell us, when they have grown older, that they really did want to have more social contact with other children.

People with ASD can appear unaware of how to get along with other people, both children and adults. They do not readily cotton on to social conventions or codes of conduct. Their social behaviour is inappropriate and clumsy. This is picked up immediately by other children, but adults can find the child's lack of reserve somewhat disarming, even charming. Adults are easily taken in by this because the child may seem mature beyond his age, which is something adults seem to value in a child.

People with ASD are unaware of how their social behaviour is seen by other people. They are oblivious as to whether or not their conversation is intrusive, welcomed or even offensive. Their conversation often turns into a sermon or a lecture, a one-way flow of words and ideas. This can become quite wearying after a while. Other children and some adults quickly learn to avoid this particular person.

Sarah lacks empathy and intuitive understanding of another person's thoughts and feelings. She has no idea why other people do not share her preferences and priorities. She is often unaware of the influences which bear on the other person's life and schedule. She does not recognize when the other person is distressed or why that might be. She does not recognize when an apology could make the other person feel better. In fact she does not even seem to understand the concept of offence and apology.

Leon seems to expect other people to know his own thoughts, opinions and experience. For example he doesn't realize that you couldn't know something because you were not there at the time it happened.

Oliver needs an excessive amount of reassurance. He prefers everything to stay the same or to conform to his preferences and dislikes. This makes him especially intolerant of change. Small departures from normal routine can result in a major meltdown. This can be as seemingly trivial as driving home from school by a different route or making a quick detour to the supermarket on the way to a familiar destination. He prefers to stay exactly where he is rather than face a new experience. When he is persuaded to try something new he is on edge and ready to retreat at the slightest provocation. He often frankly refuses to try something new. However, once he is finally engaged in this new activity he can enjoy his experience immensely but without making the connection that his refusal was illogical.

Maria is unable to exercise subtlety in how she expresses her emotions. Her distress, or rage, or affection or laughter is out of proportion to the situation. She can throw the most spectacular tantrums – meltdowns – which can go on for what seems like ages, sometimes one or two hours, or more. And then, when it is all over, she seems totally unaware of how she has just exploded. It is as if it had never happened. She has no memory of the event. She has had a clean 'reboot'.

Ahmed is unable to control the level of how he expresses his emotions in different situations. For example he does not seem to understand that it is appropriate to use self-restraint in some situations. He appears totally uninhibited in public places or with people he doesn't know when other children of his age have already learnt that this is not acceptable.

Laura has no interest in participating in competitive sports or games and communal activities. She is not interested in comparing her performance with that of other people. She has no interest in how well other children do. She is indifferent to the idea of self-improvement. It would never occur to her that other people enjoy being competitive. So why bother?

Jacob is indifferent to other people's expectations. His expectations arise from his own interests and motivations. He is not aware of, or interested in, current fads or fashions. He does not seek to expand his experience by following the lead other children and adults may show him. The status quo is just fine.

Nick makes a literal interpretation of language. For example, when asked what colour a banana is he replied that it is white. Most of us would have answered that it is yellow because of our loose use of language. If we had asked him what colour the outside of a banana skin is he would, of course, have given us the answer we were expecting.

Shelley does not understand metaphor. For example if you say 'pull your socks up' that is exactly what she will do. If you say she 'has ants in her pants' be ready for mild panic. If you want her to change her behaviour you will need to state precisely the behaviour you want. Metaphorical phrases such as 'makes me climb the wall', 'if looks could kill', 'I could eat a horse', 'go the extra mile', and so on, are a waste of breath. You will have to learn to say 'I do not like what you are doing', 'you are angry', 'I am very hungry' and 'do your best'.

Children with ASD may have an unusual tone of voice or way of speaking. They may speak with an unusual accent or in a monotone, without emphasis on key words. They may sound like a robot, prattling on without pausing for effect or to see if you are interested. You may find it difficult to get a word in edgewise, to use a metaphor. They will not know that you have something to say on the subject. They will not be interested in your point of view. It's all about them.

Similarly, their speech may be over-precise or pedantic. They may emphasize certain consonants in certain words. They may talk as if they are reading from a book or an encyclopaedia.

In conversation they may seem uninterested in the other side of the conversation. It would not occur to them that the other person might have opinions on their subject or know things that might interest them. They return to the topic of their diatribe if interrupted or if the other person tries to change the subject. If the conversation gets stuck, they rarely know how to keep up the momentum by changing the subject or asking a question of or about the other person.

In meeting someone, having a conversation and in groups Briony tends to use much less eye contact than you would expect. The mention of her name does not attract eye contact. She does not look at you for reassurance or encouragement. She does not check out your face to see how you are reacting to her. She does not know how to interpret the facial expressions of other people. She misses out on all the non-verbal cues that accompany human interaction. Her own facial expressions do not match where she is in a conversation. For example she will often assume a baffled, blank smile when she is in trouble. This can be interpreted as oppositional and lead to more trouble – her facial expression often being seen as 'an insolent grin'.

Children with ASD often read mainly for information. They may be an avid reader of science books, encyclopaedias, maps, timetables, catalogues or single-topic books. Their interests may be quite outside the range of topics one would expect for their age. At six years of age, for example, Harry can tell you all about how chlorophyl is involved in photosynthesis. They usually avoid fictional books, especially those that rely on talking about people and their relationships.

They may have an exceptional memory for facts or events. They may be able to recite timetables, capital cities, birthdays, authors or details from the past. They may know the scores of every game a favourite sports team has played and where the game took place and who was selected for that particular game. They may be able to recite the periodic table. They may know all the registration numbers of a particular aircraft fleet.

They may lack imaginative social play or interaction with other people. Even if they do enjoy imaginative play, they do not involve others. They are confused by the pretend play or social conventions of others.

They may develop elaborate routines or rituals, which must be adhered to; for example, lining up toys or other objects before bed or insisting on only wearing certain clothes. They may become upset if different foods on the dinner plate are touching each other, or if they are presented with food of a certain colour.

They may have poor physical coordination. They may have an unusual way of running or have difficulty catching a ball or skipping.

Sometimes children with ASD have an extraordinary talent in a particular area. They may be outstanding at playing a musical instrument, like the boy I know who is engrossed in the music of Mozart, or another boy who never took a piano lesson in his life but can play piano music he makes up as he goes along for four or five hours at a time. They may have extraordinary skills at mathematics or making models or computer programming. They may have exceptional computer skills and have hacked into the National Security System or the computer system of a major bank (both have actually happened). He might even be another Einstein in the making.

5

How People with ASD See the World

We are connected to the world around us by our five senses.

Which of your five senses could you live without? The answer, of course, is 'None of them, really'. Our senses serve us in so many invaluable ways. We treasure the sight of someone we love, or a landscape that is familiar. Our ability to convert sound signals emitted by other people in the form of language into two-way communication is the foundation that underpins our sense of belonging and purpose. We convert sounds we call music into inner feelings of different character and intensity that soothe or stimulate. We enjoy the aroma of a meal being prepared, or the fragrance of freshly picked flowers. We comfort ourselves through feeling warm, soft surfaces and textures; and stimulate ourselves with a plunge into a cold swimming pool.

All this we take for granted.

We turn down our awareness of what our senses tell us when it suits us to do so. We can abolish the sensation of our clothes on our body, which is a good thing, because it serves no useful purpose most of the time. We can ignore conversations going on around us when we are concentrating on doing something purposeful. We quickly get used to a new aroma and stop being aware of it.

This all falls apart if you have ASD.

Imagine that you have no control over the sensations your body experiences. Perhaps the touch of clothing on your skin is unbearably irritating and you can't switch the sensation off. It is with you all day long.

Or perhaps your vision is so sensitive that it sees everything in a magnified way that may make no sense when there is a lot going on. Might this lead to a feeling of being overwhelmed? Wouldn't you hate being taken to a shopping mall or having to go out into the playground during breaks at school?

Or perhaps voices are just noises that you cannot decipher or discriminate into meaningful communication so that you tend to be unaware of, or just ignore, people trying to talk to you or tell you things.

Maybe the texture of a certain food in your mouth triggers off feelings of distress, or maybe the thought of having to eat food of a certain colour is something you can't handle, or possibly the idea of having several different foods on the same plate is intolerable.

Perhaps the sound of splashing water in an enclosed place is stressful so that you will do anything to avoid going to a public swimming pool. You may find the sound of something quite ordinary, like a food processor or a vacuum cleaner is unbearable in the same way that 'neuro-typical' people shrink from the sound of fingernails scratching across a blackboard.

Perhaps there are certain colours that fascinate you and always capture your attention. Perhaps you become absorbed into the colour so that other things around you are overlooked, an irrelevance. How interesting these shades and tints and hues can be.

Perhaps there are many of these sensory phenomena that you find difficult to handle. Perhaps all you want to do sometimes is to find a dark quiet place to hide while your nerve endings recover – being under the bedclothes might just do the trick, or perhaps being in a room with nothing in it painted all-over sky-blue. How beautifully restful is that?

This may be the kind of world experienced by many people with ASD. It is a hostile place that drains your energy and leaves you ready to fall apart at the next, slightest sensation that makes you panic.

In a word, the world around you is stressful. STRESSFUL. And, for good measure, **STRESSFUL**!

Your world might not be the fun, sweetness-and-light, interesting, enjoyable place that 'neuro-typical' people experience.

And how come all these 'neuro-typicals' don't 'get it'? How come they expect me to have to endure all this torment all the time in their noisy, busy, full-of-surprises world? How come they don't understand that I may have had enough of this for the time being? How come they don't understand that I might just like to chill out and regain some of my balance before I have to face more of the same?

How come that when I finally snap and have a meltdown because there is just too much going on that I don't understand I get treated to a shouting display, or have to suddenly go somewhere I just hadn't been expecting. And don't they realize that they are now increasing the level of stress and overload that made me snap in the first place. Suddenly I can't think at all. Suddenly I feel blind panic. Suddenly I feel terrible.

All I need is a quiet place where I can release these nasty stress feelings, and calm myself to the point where I can think about starting over again. I would like to start over. I didn't mean to crash. I didn't intend you to feel angry with me. I just wanted to do the best I could in dealing with all this confusing input that my five senses are trying to make sense of.

It's at times like this that a bit of ritual comes in handy – very soothing, very restorative. If I flap my arms I can concentrate on that movement and block out the other stuff. Perhaps I could go through my lining-up routine. That always makes sense to me.

Wow, I can hardly wait to get home. I mostly understand being at home. Home is mostly a safe place for me where I can do what I need to do to feel better. Trouble is, when I get home I feel so stressed out that the first thing I do is have a major meltdown. I don't really know where this comes from – all I know is that by the time I get there I have just about reached the limit of what I can take. The slightest thing can now set me off. In 'neuro-typical' speak I am a loaded gun with a hair trigger – the slightest jolt is going to set me off.

I don't like this, but I have to do it. Once I have had my meltdown I feel like a new person and I can then get on with the rest of my day. I'm sorry. I can't help the fact that my meltdown may last for an eternity. It feels that way to me too, but I have learnt, and I hope you have too, that afterwards I will be OK. When I feel calm again you can talk to me and I can try to listen to you.

I think what has happened is that everyone has been trying to run Windows programs on my Apple computer. Often this results in me just freezing up. If I quit the program I was running before you tried your Windows keystrokes on me, I can probably reload and get going again. But sometimes there are so many Windows keystrokes going on, or you just happen to hit on one critical key that makes me crash. You can call it a meltdown if you like.

Who knows what will happen next? My screen could fill with gobbledegook or perhaps just random images or whatever. Now the only thing that will fix me is a total reboot. I will need to switch off completely. I need to de-power. I need to wait until any residual current has dissipated.

Now I am ready to restart and reboot. Now I am up and running. Everything is as it was before. There is nothing on my hard drive or in my short-term memory other than Apple stuff. All that Windows stuff has disappeared, but I don't know that, because I don't remember – it got wiped off my memory chip. Now I am as good as new. This is a good time for us to talk about how I behave. It's a good time for you to give me the opportunity to talk about different ways I could do things to be more effective. And it's a good time to get me to talk about how I see things so that you can understand me better.

I'm sure you could understand me better if you could allow me to try to explain to you why I behave as I do. Life would be so much better for both of us if you could re-interpret my behaviour in a new and more understanding light.

If you try carefully and use small bits of computer code at a time, you might be able to write little programs in Apple code that will allow me to create small applications that run as if they are Windows programs. If you are careful about how you do this, and if you avoid too many lines of Windows code at a time, and if you let me quit or reboot when I need to, I think you will be surprised at how much more like a Windows computer I could appear to you. I will still be an Apple computer underneath, and I will always be an Apple computer, and I will always prefer to run Apples programs, especially those fabulous graphics and music programs that come so easily to me. I may never really be good at word processing and spreadsheets that Windows computers can excel at. But you may be able to fill my desktop with a useful collection of little Windows look-alikes that we call widgets, or apps, if you want to be really up to date, so that I can do lots of useful Windows stuff, only not quite as quickly or fluently as a Windows computer.

By the way, I am not your enemy. I am trying really hard to do my best to please you. It's just that you are doing all this Windows stuff that really confuses me. I would truly like to do my best to meet your expectations, if you would only try to understand what is going on in my brain. I have a suggestion for you if you could take the time to slow down and listen to me.

If you were to catch me in one of my quiet, unstressed times and ask me how I think I could begin to fit better into your world, I could give you heaps of ideas about what works for me. Perhaps it's a matter of getting down to my level, using my name to catch my attention, and then explaining to me exactly what you would like me to do. If you ask me to repeat your instructions then we will both know whether I have understood correctly. Or perhaps you could write down the schedule somewhere I can see it so that I know what to expect next. If you ask me about any situation you see as problematic I will give you my honest opinion about what will work best — and don't worry: I have ASD so I always tell the truth and never try deception.

By the way, did I tell you about how good I am at seeing all the subtle shades of blue there are? Blue is such an interesting and absorbing colour. I can see blue a mile off. I am fascinated by how the iridescence of blue attracts my attention. I could feel really comfortable surrounded by just blue. There needn't be a horizon, just endless blue, and if the shades and hues could be constantly changing I would be really happy. Just thought I'd share that with you to give you a taste of how different I can be, apropos of nothing.

6

Stress and Anxiety

Perhaps by now you are beginning to get the idea that the person with ASD experiences feelings of stress and anxiety nearly all the time. I cannot emphasize this enough. If you have ASD you have stress. If you have ASD you feel on edge. If you have ASD you feel anxious. What you need to deal with this is a life of predictable stability.

It's good to know that you won't be disturbed. It's good to know that at a certain time a meal will arrive, assuming, of course, that you have no hang-ups about food. It's good to know that you can do what appeals to you for as long as it appeals to you. It's good to know that there won't be any surprises – Yeah, right!

Of course, life is not like that – unless you are a hermit (do hermits have ASD?). You have to fit in with the rest of us, and many of us are comfortable with change, surprises and disappointments, even if we don't like living life on the edge! We take the need for change in our stride. If something unexpected comes up we cope. We make last-minute changes to suit changing circumstances without batting an eyelid.

Anxiety and brain plasticity

When we use the term 'brain plasticity' we refer to the intrinsic capacity of the brain to remodel itself by preserving useful connections, discarding useless connections and forming new connections. Brain plasticity is the basis of learning, remembering and developing.

We usually look at the concept of brain plasticity in a favourable light. Learning and development are useful. Memory is a good thing. Let's have all the brain plasticity we can get.

But hang on a minute – perhaps the brain can learn and remodel itself in unhelpful ways.

It certainly can. The brain of a person who has experienced neglect and abuse throughout childhood models itself differently from that of a person who grows up in a safe and nurturing home. These differences last a lifetime. We all know this. And what's more it is relatively easy to recognize abuse and neglect and easy to recognize a happy family when we see one. So we can potentially do something about a bad situation in order to try to get a better outcome in the long run.

But what if the brain is remodelling itself in an unhelpful way and we don't have a clue that this is going on? Would that be a lost opportunity? Would we later say that we wished we had known so that we could have done something about it? Yes, of course we would.

The scientific community is becoming increasingly aware that chronic anxiety states in adults often have their root cause in unrecognized chronic anxiety in childhood. The anxiety becomes wired into the brain because of brain plasticity. This is not good. This is not what we want. This is definitely not what we need.

What we need is an increased awareness that chronic anxiety in a child might be there, right under our noses, and we just don't see it. We certainly don't do anything about it. This unawareness allows the chronic anxiety to go on and on. It allows the chronic anxiety to lead to behaviours that prompt adults and other children to act in ways that make the anxiety worse. Can you see a downward spiral here?

Let's be on the lookout for chronic anxiety in children with ASD, and let's make sure we deal with it as aggressively and positively as we can.

And while we are at it let's generalize our concern to other children and include loss of self-esteem, chronic depression and chronic neglect and abuse in our list of things to look for and do something about.

7

And Now for the Good News

Having ASD is not all bad news. In fact many people with ASD are among the most interesting people you will ever meet. That doesn't mean they can't be challenging, of course!

To start with you might think of them as being eccentric or weird. You now know that this is because they handle social relationships differently from most people. They can seem aloof or appear to have a one-track mind. You now know that they may perceive the world around them in their own unique way. What you may learn, however, is that many of them have amazing talents and capabilities.

Mozart is said to have had Asperger syndrome – many consider him to have been the greatest musical genius of all time. Einstein is thought to have had Asperger syndrome – he gave us the theory of relativity and a number of possibly more important mathematical, astronomic and physics concepts. You will have met crazy musicians, quirky novelists, mad scientists, and so on, in your own life. Chances are that many of them have ASD but you just didn't realize it at the time. And you may know someone who is an accountant or an engineer. These are two professions that are known to attract people who have ASD, but you might never know.

If you have had someone with ASD recently diagnosed in your family, there is a good chance that you already know a relative who also has ASD but you just didn't realize it. If so, you may be in luck, because the person newly diagnosed may just get on very well with the relative with ASD. They can understand each other in ways that elude the rest of us. They deal with facts, not feelings. They simplify things in their friendship. They don't bother with the social niceties that can complicate relationships in families. They don't talk unless they have something important to say about something concrete. They don't do guile, intrigue or nuance. What you see and hear is what you get, plain and simple. That is so no-stress!

Some of the most prominent mathematicians, scientists, musicians, artists, engineers, astronomers and computer experts have ASD. Some totally unknown people with ASD are highly productive in their work, like the gentleman with Asperger syndrome who lives in one room of his parents' house in my hometown in New Zealand, seldom bathing or shaving and never going out. He stays in his room at one end of the house writing computer programs for the Massachusetts Institute of Technology (MIT). He is doing what he is good at and what he enjoys. He is avoiding everything he dislikes. The average person might frown on hearing about him. But for him, things just don't get any better. He is untroubled by the world outside and happy in his own.

When I meet a young person with ASD for the first time I am no longer surprised if I find that the father has similar behavioural differences and endured a childhood of being ridiculed, marginalized and unreasonably punished for being unable to comply with the demands of the day. But he survived and is now working as a computer programmer in a back room somewhere, or rebuilding helicopters in a hangar somewhere, or doing the lighting for a stage production somewhere, or undertaking scientific research somewhere. He serves as a living testimony to the fact that having ASD is not necessarily a barrier to getting on in life.

Now that we know so much more about ASD we can assist in this process and ensure that each person with ASD gets a better chance of surviving and becoming the person he is capable of being.

Part II

ASD – What Can We Do About It?

8

Guiding Principles

So now what?

Well, by now you should be beginning to understand what ASD is all about and what it might be like to be someone whose brain is wired to give them ASD.

Let's now look at some of the guiding principles that will help us work with and assist the person with ASD get on better. You might find it useful to briefly read each section first in order to get a rough overview. You can return to any section at a later date to review the principles and see how you might apply them to your situation. Remember these are guidelines and as such they are supposed to be flexible. As long as you stick to the basic concepts you can modify your approach to fit your situation.

We will discuss these strategies under the following headings.

- Remember, this person is hard-wired differently.

- Seek alternative explanations for behaviour.

- Make sure that everybody involved understands.

- Listen to what the person with ASD tells you.

- Listen to what the family tells you.

- Make sure you have the right Chair of the Board.

- Create structure and predictability.

- Anticipate and deal with transitions.

- Create self-help options.

- Compensate for lack of self-directed learning.

- Work through strengths, by-pass weaknesses.

- Abandon the standard curriculum.

- Teach skills for life.

- Use visual approaches to learning whenever possible.

- Stay concrete: avoid metaphor, irony, sarcasm, cynicism, etc.

- Reinforce teaching of social skills.

- Deal with stress.

- Remember that not much learning occurs when there is stress.

- Remember that punishment does not produce learning.

- Avoid power struggles.

These principles demand that we are prepared to change our thinking and our instinctive behaviour. This may well make us feel unnatural and awkward. We are going to have to go out on a limb and rethink our strategies.

This may be made even more difficult because we are going to have to explain to those around us why we have abandoned conventional methods. There is every chance that others will think we are crazy, that we have lost the plot. It will be hard enough just having to concentrate on doing things differently without having to spend time and energy dealing with the 'world experts' around us who think we are doing it all wrong.

What is needed is often counter-intuitive to those who do not understand the true nature of ASD. So for a while we may feel a bit lonely, a bit unsupported.

At times like this it is often helpful to have the phone number of one of your local support organizations handy. You can find these on the internet or in the telephone directory – look under 'autism' or 'autistic' in the directory or do a search with 'autism support' or something similar if you are on the internet.

Let's now take a look in closer detail at these important strategies and principles you will need to master.

9

Remember, This Person is Hard-wired Differently

Remember the computer analogy? Do I need to say more?

The person *we are interested in* has ASD and his brain is hard-wired differently to most of the rest of us. This results in differences in the broad realms of communication, in social interaction and in interests. If you need to refresh your memory on this you could go back to the beginning chapters.

My point here is that it is so easy to forget this important principle. It is so easy to slip back into our natural mental framework which we use to make assumptions about other people, what they are thinking, what they are doing and why they are thinking what they are thinking which is causing them to do what they are doing. After all, this is what comes naturally and easily to us. We do it in a flash.

But when we are dealing with somebody who has ASD we must be on constant guard against this natural tendency to be 'neuro-typical'. Because it is not natural for us to have to consider that someone else could be hard-wired differently we will often forget to make the mental adjustment necessary when we are talking to and working with someone with ASD.

However, if you stick at it this will quickly become second nature. You may slip back into the old thinking mould from time to time. That's OK. You will be reminded at the next meltdown.

Just as importantly we will probably forget, at least to begin with, that stress and anxiety will be just below the surface trying to make themselves known to us by producing all kinds of behaviours and responses that may baffle us.

This leads us on to perhaps the most important principle of all.

10

Seek Alternative Explanations for Behaviour

First, and above all, STOP and consider that what you are seeing as unacceptable or unhelpful behaviour is almost certainly not what you think it is.

'Don't just do something, stand there!'

Give yourself time to think through what the behaviour you have just observed is trying to communicate. After all, behaviour is a powerful means of communication. If someone who is 'neuro-typical' – a Windows computer – throws a tantrum, you are likely to assume that what is being communicated is opposition to what is being asked for or frustration at not getting their own way. It is the expression of a strong personal preference – 'My way or the highway'.

So we interpret the same behaviour in someone who has ASD as communicating resistance, frustration, disrespect, defiance, me-against-you, or whatever.

But if people with ASD throw a tantrum are they trying to communicate the same opposition or defiance? Could it be that at this point their computer has just crashed, because the last keystroke was just one too many? Did they understand why you wanted what you wanted? Did you give them warning that a change was about to take place? Did you ask for something that was not predictable? Is this utter confusion?

Now is the time to go with the flow and provide space and time for things to settle. A bit of quiet may help at this point. If you try to intervene to settle things down you are likely to make things worse, not better. It's OK to feel helpless, even if you usually see yourself as the 'Master of the Universe' most of the time. And it also helps if you can avoid personalizing the situation. This is not about you, your mastery, your authority or your lack thereof. It is about a person with ASD having a crisis. This crisis is not directed at you. It is about a computer that just crashed and needs to be shut down and then rebooted.

So if in doubt, walk out. Back off. Chill out. Make a cup of tea. Do anything that is not getting more involved.

Once things have calmed down and rebooting has taken place we can talk things through dispassionately.

Revisiting the events that preceded the crash is a waste of time and energy. Instead you could talk about things in general, such as how to have a really good meltdown. Where is the best place for this? What would be OK to do in a meltdown? What is not OK in a meltdown? Meltdowns are inevitable, so let's get really good at having meltdowns that are safe and do no harm.

Remember that this person tends to see the world in a concrete framework. He does not understand social niceties. He is not very good at turn taking. He speaks whenever he has something to say. He can be highly analytical and uninhibited. He may have amazing skills of deconstruction, meaning that he can break things down into tiny detail and then point out any discrepancies or defects in logic or consistency that he discovers. This can seem confrontational if you are the subject being treated to this forensic examination. You may react in an emotional or defensive way.

Because of this he can become confused and upset if you don't do exactly what you told him you would do. If you change routine without warning, he becomes distressed and anxious. He will not see your logic.

If you say something that contradicts something you said earlier, he will point this out to you even in situations, like high-school classrooms, where this is not a good move – he is likely to be thought of as showing lack of respect and being out to make a nuisance of himself. The rest of the class know it is better to stay quiet, even if they pick up on the same inconsistency. The same young man can quickly gain a reputation as a troublemaker. The more the school community becomes aware of his 'attitude', the more readily will his behaviour be thought of as troublemaking.

Or, now that he is more mature, our young man has learnt how to modulate his prior meltdowns from out-and-out lack of control and replace them by a short demonstration of distress, like throwing his test paper back at the teacher when the teacher has decided on a surprise exam. At a time like this it pays to remember that people with ASD don't 'do' surprises. If you had told him yesterday that there would be a test today there would have been no problem. He would be ready.

Now it is a real battle to persuade everybody that they may have got this young man wrong. This is quite a challenge. Entrenched values and beliefs are at stake here. This is the time for a bit of continuing professional development and, with any luck, providing education about ASD to school staff and parents and students will allow them to develop a new approach to the young man in question.

In doing this we must all remind ourselves to stay concrete. We need simple statements of what is acceptable and what is not acceptable.

'Show respect for your teacher', 'Do not do naughty things in class', 'Behave yourself' are examples of non-concrete expression. Statements like this only confuse the person with ASD.

'You may smile at your teacher', 'Do not talk about your teacher's hair', 'Do not speak during a class unless the teacher has asked you to speak' are all concrete statements which are likely to help the person with ASD.

11

Make Sure That Everybody Involved Understands

A veil of secrecy often surrounds the diagnosis of a person with ASD. Perhaps this is OK if we are talking about an adult with ASD. Secrecy, or confidentiality, is often preferred by the parents of a young person who has ASD. And the rest of us are usually quite happy to go along with this – it is the easier option and requires no active effort. We just get on with life as if nothing were happening.

There is a better way.

The problem with this approach is that it is blindingly obvious to everybody involved that the person we are talking about *is* different. We may not be able to put our finger on exactly what the difference is, but we are aware of it nonetheless. This awareness will tend to lead us to discriminatory actions. We may tend to avoid the person in question. We may paint her as a source of amusement or ridicule. We may develop prejudice against her. These and other similar responses are natural when we feel uncomfortable with the person.

However, suppose someone told us about why this person is the way she is. There is a strong possibility we might see her in a different light. We might even begin to admire and respect her for facing what the world throws at her. We might be motivated to get alongside her and find ways of helping. We might begin to include her in what we do instead of shunning her.

This can be a positive force, especially in schools.

Whole-of-school approach

I strongly believe and advocate that all efforts should be made to adopt a 'whole-of-school' approach in meeting the challenges faced by the child with ASD. Of course the family need to be comfortable about this before we start. However, once family members begin to get their heads around the diagnosis and its implications they can usually see the benefit of this approach because of how it will improve things for their child.

Up until now this child may have behaved in many un-helpful ways because of his hard-wired lack of understanding about how to get along in groups, and because of high stress and anxiety levels. He may have done things deemed unacceptable. At worst he may have threatened or hit out at someone during a moment of acute distress and anxiety and been labelled as having an 'anger problem' or being 'aggressive'.

Among other things we need to be sure that the adults understand the difference between acute anxiety and premeditated aggression.

I use the analogy of a cat here – when a cat is being aggressive, stalking a bird perhaps, it moves slowly and stealthily until at the final moment it pounces. This is an impressive display of self-control and mastery. However, when a cat is cornered and feels acute fear and anxiety it hisses, arches its back, raises the fur on its back, bares its teeth and claws and spits. This looks aggressive, doesn't it? However, what we are now seeing is a 'fight or flight' situation caused by acute anxiety and not by aggression.

Our young person with ASD and high levels of anxiety often finds himself in a 'fight or flight' situation. His response is just as automatic as the cornered cat. Aggression or anger is never intended. What we are seeing is stress and confusion. If he loses it or hits out, please remember this and look for alternative explanations for behaviour.

However, you can readily understand why the adult can get it wrong. The consequence of behaviour interpreted as aggression or anger is that the child is disciplined and sooner or later begins to be seen by the adults around him as a big problem. This naturally affects how the adults come to behave towards the child, and gradually the child's classmates pick up on this and start behaving in the same way towards him, usually by excluding him or by teasing and bullying him. In other words, the approach modelled by the teacher is reflected in the behaviour of the children. Things go from bad to worse. Our young man becomes increasingly anxious, which serves only to increase the behaviour that gets him into trouble.

This demands sensitive and informed intervention. Depending on the situation and the degree to which the child is seen as a problem, we may need to start with the school principal or head teacher and the school board if there is one. We need to start at the top because we are going to be asking for special consideration, which may be at odds with standard school policy and with the general view of the child. The aim here is to ensure that everybody understands the nature of ASD, its hard-wired differences, how that affects behaviour and why we need to permit exceptions to rules.

All members of the teaching staff need to understand the true nature and implications of ASD, because we need their support and understanding if we are to create special circumstances for this person. Once the teachers start modelling new behaviours towards a child who was previously in trouble all the time, the rest of the students begin to notice.

So now, as far as possible, fellow students need to be educated about ASD at a level they can understand. At the very least this should include students in the same class. Extending this to a wider group of students would be even better – perhaps to all the students of the same age or older.

This 'whole-of-school' approach is important because we need to acknowledge that everyone who comes into contact with the person with ASD very quickly picks up on the fact that something is different. It is respectful to acknowledge and validate these perceptions and to explain them. The result is that suspicion and discomfort are replaced by understanding, concern and a willingness to accommodate rather than exclude. So now we have the adults and the children all singing from the same hymn sheet and combining to create a powerfully supportive environment for our child. I call this 'moral congruence' and, of course, it can work both ways, as we saw earlier.

Which situation would you prefer?

Taking a 'whole-of-school' approach can be a daunting exercise the first time it is put into action in a school that hitherto was uninformed about ASD. However, the benefits greatly reward the effort involved. This trail blazing makes it so much easier for the next child with ASD who comes along, and for all those involved with her development and education.

Before long you will have a ASD-friendly school.

To illustrate this here is an email from a teacher to a parent of a child with ASD. This child had been excluded from school for a short time because of behaviour interpreted as aggression. After a review of the implications of his diagnosis of ASD and some learning about ASD the teacher, in consultation with the parents, took the risk of discussing the child's situation with the full class at a time when the child was not present.

See what you think about this email the teacher sent to the parents that day.

> I thought that I would let you know that as a class we discussed ******'s behaviour this afternoon. The general feeling from the children is that they are very concerned for him at the moment. They feel that he is out of the room a lot and they are worried that he might not feel as much a part of the team because of it. Comments were made that suggested that he seemed a little sad. Many people felt that he was trying harder as part of group work and that in the playground he seemed less aggressive.
>
> We discussed strategies that we felt were fair for him and so as not to stop the learning so much. The children know that he loves his book and is hooked on it and they suggested that when he is being very disruptive he should sit on the couch and read. Tomorrow we are all going to do everything we can to support ****** and in the words of the children 'help him be a high flyer'.
>
> They felt that his muffins today were extremely kind and seemed like an apology for the past behaviour so everybody wants him to succeed in his goal and intends to help him.
>
> I thought that this was a positive response and demonstrated to me that the children consider ****** a friend and part of the team. It is important to celebrate the positives like this.

Wow! What a brilliant step towards becoming a ASD-friendly school. And what great teacher – parent communication.

12

Listen to What the Person with ASD Tells You

If you recall earlier chapters, you will remember how differently the person with ASD can see and experience the world around her. You will recall that her sensory experiences can be spectacularly different from how we experience the same world. She may become stressed and anxious over what we would see as something of no importance. And when she is stressed she is unable to learn

So how do we handle this?

We have already discussed the importance of seeking alternative and appropriate explanations for the behaviours we see. The only person who can really explain this to us is the child herself. Of course, many young people with ASD are not able to do this because of the intrinsic impairments in communication which are part-and-parcel of their differences. In these cases we are left with trial and error in finding the best way of responding to stressed behaviour.

However, the majority of children we are dealing with can tell us perfectly well what bothers them, what works for them and what doesn't work for them. We need to catch them in a quiet space when they are relaxed. We need to get down to their eye level and use concrete language to discuss the pressure points they see in their day-to-day lives. Once we get used to doing this we will likely discover that this young person is wiser than we might think. They may be able to give us many pointers on how we could do things differently in order to achieve the same outcome without all the fuss.

We can start by telling them about something that they must do, and why this is necessary. We can then ask them to talk to us about this. They will probably stonewall us to start with. That's OK. We can then begin to talk about ways they might be able to do the task in question and still remain comfortable. We do this by asking questions about what might work. As long as we avoid putting pressure on them we can continue to widen the list of options. With each option we need to talk about what the result will be so that there are no surprises. Gradually we can develop a sense of movement in the right direction

Our natural tendency is to use word pictures when we talk with other people. Remember, the person with ASD is likely to be highly visual so we need to use visual pictures whenever we can to reinforce our messages.

One of the features of the thinking patterns of people with ASD is that they are honest. They will not try to deceive you. They do not understand guile, intrigue, subterfuge or deception. They think in concrete terms. They will give it to you straight. This is a tremendously valuable safeguard when we recruit children to advise us on what works best, how to make things less stressful for them. We can rest assured that they will not see this as an unexpected opportunity to take advantage of what 'neuro-typical' people might see as leniency or unreasonable accommodation.

13

Listen to What the Family Tells You

The child's family have also become world experts on their particular child. Admittedly they probably didn't undertake teacher training and have no experience of hands-on classroom management. However, in this situation the family has an advantage which you can turn into your own if you only take time to listen to their advice, their insights and their concerns.

Many families report that their experience with schools results in their feeling that their knowledge of the child is not something the school is interested in. They feel belittled, undervalued and humiliated when their concerns and knowledge are not taken seriously and when the school persists in seeing their child in an inappropriate light. We end up with a polarized relationship between home and school.

What a pity!

How much better it would be if the teacher did not feel threatened by the mother of this child. Is it possible for this teacher to see past her defensiveness and open her mind to the possibility that she could learn something useful from the mother, or that perhaps her own professional development would benefit by getting informed about ASD? Many teachers have told me that they appreciate learning about

ASD, not only for its intrinsic value but also because they find it liberating to be able to see all the roadblocks for what they are, and now it is OK to think about a few detours.

14

Make Sure You Have the Right Chair of the Board

In the context of this section of the book I like to think of a child as a commercial enterprise, a company. Let's call her 'Your Child Limited' or 'Your Child plc' or 'Your Child Inc.'.

All companies have to be registered and all companies are required to have a Board of Directors. The company is required to have annual meetings and consider resolutions necessary for planning its business. Directors are appointed to oversee the management and operation of the company. Their knowledge and judgement are important to the success of the enterprise. We don't appoint someone to the board of a mining company who has no knowledge of mining or mineralogy or marketing, for example. We prefer to ensure that all directors on the board are knowledgeable and will provide value.

This enterprise called 'Your Child Limited' has a Board of Directors. Sitting at the board table you are likely to find at least one but usually both of the child's parents. That's usually as far as it goes. Grandparents might get a permanent seat at the board table – but probably not.

When the question of the child's education comes up, the role of the board is usually restricted to awarding a 'management contract' for the child's education to one of the local schools. It is assumed that the school has the necessary knowledge, skills and resources to provide an appropriate academic education for the child. The school has thereby replaced the parents on the board in all matters that have to do with schooling. The school principal has become the 'de facto' Chair of the Board. He delegates responsibility for the child's education to the teacher or teachers and receives periodic reports on how the child is doing and shares this with the parents.

This usually works out just fine. The school, the principal, the teachers, the curriculum all work on shared assumptions about what teaching methods and what teaching subject matter are appropriate for all children in general. The system has evolved over the years by review and improvement to be what it is today, designed to meet the needs of both the student and the society in which the child is growing up.

However, this won't work if 'Your Child Inc.' happens to be in the business of ASD. We cannot assume that the school has the knowledge, skills and resources to allow it to undertake the 'management contract' for the academic education of the child with ASD. It is even possible, if not likely, that the school principal may not have the qualifications in ASD to be Chair of the Board, and that the teachers to whom he delegates are just as likely to lack sufficient knowledge and understanding of ASD to be able to optimize the child's education.

In this situation, it becomes necessary for the child's own board of directors (the parents) to move into the school and co-opt the school staff to their board in a shared planning structure. Ideally the Chair of the Board should be the student herself – after all, she is undoubtedly the person best qualified to advise the board on what will work, what will not work and what needs to be done to create the best learning environment for her. Failing that the next best option is for one or both of the parents to take the chair.

This can be quite a departure from 'normal' ways of doing things in many schools. But perhaps the 'whole-of-school' approach we talked about earlier may prepare the school to risk it. It will pay off. Once we have the knowledge and advice from the child and the parents, and permit them to direct proceedings we have laid the foundation for getting the very best results achievable.

To illustrate all this, you may like to know of a young man with Asperger syndrome who became too anxious to attend school. The school came up with all kinds of strategies to deal with this. None of them worked. At a meeting of professionals and the boy's parents the school agreed to the concept of the boy becoming the 'Chairman of his Board of Directors'. He was given the privilege of telling the school what he thought would work best for him. The school responded magnificently. After a year or so of part-time attendance to do the things he chose to do at school and the remainder of his learning at home he now attends school full-time again. His curriculum is heavily biased towards music; his driving passion in life is Mozart, which he plays on the piano whenever he can. He has dispensation to go to the music room instead of the playground during school breaks. This is enormously relaxing and restoring for him and gives him the chance to reboot before his next class. As he grows older and matures he is able gradually to extend his wider experience at school and is now interested in learning some basic social skills.

And, of course, he has been permitted to abandon the strict requirements of the standard curriculum – his career goal is to become a musician, which is achievable without slavishly sticking to the standard curriculum. He is a member of a local music group, which gives him the chance of extending his social network and the confidence to perform as a member of a team.

Overall he is now very much happier and competent than he was in the days when he had no seat at the boardroom table. His academic learning has accelerated and his musical performances are stunning. He has become transformed from a misfit into a school hero. Last time I saw him he was playing Beethoven's Third Piano Concerto with our local orchestra!

15

Create Structure and Predictability

For most of us life is an adventure to be lived to the full, and the fuller the better. We thrive on variety and get bored with monotony. We love trying new things, and for us a change is as good as a rest.

It is hard to imagine that all this is exactly what scares the living daylights out of the person with ASD.

The person with ASD would like things to stay the same.

Monotony would be just fine, thank you. That is my preference, but don't forget that for me monotony is not monotonous.

If I can't have monotony and predictability I would like to know exactly what is going to happen and when it will happen. I like to know in advance if there is to be a change. Sure, this might make me anxious, but if you explain to me what the change will look like that would help. Don't think that by withholding information about a change this will help me cope better. I don't like surprises.

And don't be surprised if I protest about having to do something new. That's just how I am and it would be good if you didn't take it personally. Don't let my initial resistance put you off because there is a good chance that I might actually enjoy this new activity.

What works best for me is a fairly simple schedule in which one day is the same as another. I need a schedule which I can rely on to occur exactly as planned. I would like it best if the schedule is written up on a whiteboard somewhere we can all see it. The kitchen would be a good place for this.

I would like to rely on everybody sticking to the schedule. If you say we are going somewhere after school, don't expect me to be happy if you decide to go to the supermarket on the way there if this wasn't in the schedule. I might become stressed by this and have a meltdown. These unexpected things are hard for me to deal with, especially just after a full day at school, which has already freaked me out, if you must know.

And don't forget that if I am having a meltdown because of this surprise change to the published schedule any amount of reasoning will not help me cope right now.

It would be OK to talk about it after I have recovered (rebooted) though – this might help me deal with it better next time. It might also help you to remember to give me advanced notice next time, or rearrange your schedule in order to keep to mine.

16

Anticipate and Deal with Transitions

The person with ASD often has difficulty moving from one thing to another. In the case of children this shows up as stress when a transition is necessary. In adults we see people getting 'stuck' and not being able to figure out for themselves how to move on.

All children quickly learn that when an adult says 'in five minutes' or 'soon' this can mean anything from 'straightaway' to 'never'. The child quickly learns that an adult's conception of time is approximate at best and totally unreliable at worst.

The best way of overcoming this is to use objective measures of time. It is better to say something like 'We will stop when the big hand is on the twelve' or 'Let's set the timer for five minutes and when it goes off that will be the signal to stop'.

So managing the stress of transitions works best when we incorporate the idea of structure we discussed above and using objective measures of time to warn that a predicted change in activity is about to happen.

For example, we are going to have to stop playing on the computer in order to eat supper. We could consult our child and ask him to come up with a plan that we could all use to get us through this troublesome transition. He may be reluctant at first, but we might end up with something like:

1.   Our whiteboard timetable clearly shows 'computer time' and then 'logging off computer' and then 'suppertime'.

2.   Five-minute signal that 'computer time' will be ending so please stop what you are doing and get ready to close down your programme.

3.   One-minute signal to start logging out.

4.   Switch computer off and move to table.

As we have already discussed we can increase the effectiveness of such a transition if we consult the people involved and ask what they think would be the best way of moving from one activity to another – we will get the best procedure and we are more likely to get adherence to 'their' plan.

Some transitions will, from time to time, involve a brand new experience. For example, we might have enrolled our child in tae kwan do. We have talked about tae kwan do and shown pictures or You-Tube clips of someone doing it. We have explained who will be there and hopefully shown a picture of the tutor. We might then drive to the venue and look at it from the outside. Perhaps we could also go inside and look around. We might do this without the child and take some photos we could then show him later. The more we can help the child know in advance what is likely to be involved, the easier it will be for him.

A stitch in time saves nine (another metaphor).

17

Create Self-help Options

Life may not be a bed of roses for our young person with ASD. We already know how stress and anxiety loom in the awareness of this person. What is much more difficult to know is how stress and anxiety is building up at any point in time. We may be totally unaware that our person is about to reach 'meltdown'. By the time this occurs we have, of course, missed the boat. This is not our fault – we would have no way of knowing, after all.

So again we have to fall back on the person herself. She is aware of how she is feeling. Who better to know when relief is needed?

What we need is a plan for stress reduction. Let's choose a quiet moment when she is comfortable and able to talk freely. Now we can talk about the things she feels when she is about to have a meltdown.

How would it be if you could choose something to do to make yourself feel better and calmer? What might that be? Perhaps you would like to walk to a quiet place in the library and stay there for a few minutes and come back when you feel ready. Perhaps we could make somewhere for you to use in the classroom. Perhaps all you need to do is take the seat in the corner and look at a book, or cover your ears, or whatever works for you. Perhaps we need to find a fridge box or something like that and put some soft things like a pillow or a furry throw inside so that you could retreat there when you need to. Perhaps having a favourite strokey soft toy in your bag that you could reach into and stroke is all you need.

Now that you have a plan, we need to put it into action so that whenever she feels she needs to she has the freedom to withdraw until she is ready to rejoin. Don't worry that this privilege might be abused. She really would prefer to be with the class and as soon as she is ready she will return.

Another helpful intervention is to make a stress meter for the child with a moveable arrow she can use to tell us how anxious she is feeling at any point in time. She has control of this and she can communicate where she is at quietly and unambiguously. She may like to make the stress meter herself to her specifications.

Of course, all her classmates are in on this, because we have explained to them that they are right – she is different, but that's OK. She needs one or two things in the class to help her cope and learn better so we will be doing one or two unusual but necessary things. As we said before, most kids want to help, so they will be happy to go along with this. Furthermore, this will provide priceless learning for them which they will carry with them well into adulthood.

18

Compensate for Lack of Self-directed Learning

Most children are driven to learn by play and exploration. Initially this is done in isolation and then gradually over time children learn how to do this in groups. This extends learning to encompass social learning and purposeful social interaction.

Children with ASD are usually just the opposite. They may spend hours doing one thing repetitively, over and over. Their repertoire of play activities may be very narrow. They may not be motivated to involve themselves with other children or adults. They may actively seek solitude.

The degree of restriction varies a great deal, but what is important is to recognize that compared to their 'neurotypical' classmates there are significant degrees of impairment, however subtle these may be. If left to their own devices, young people with ASD may tend to withdraw or, because of their awkwardness, be shunned by their classmates.

When this happens they often gravitate to the edge of groups of older children whom they watch rather than join, or to groups of younger children whose social maturity is more akin to their own.

In the same vein, intellectual exploration may be restricted by an overwhelming fascination with a particular topic or activity.

It is up to us to constantly 'nudge' young people with ASD to broaden and extend their abilities and experiences. It is not unusual for adults with ASD to make the point that they now wish that greater efforts had been made to push them into a wider range of experiences and teach them a wider range of skills.

Perhaps the most useful area in which we can nudge the person is in the acquisition of social skills. It is possible to teach these especially if you stay concrete. There are several good books out there specifically aimed at doing this. They work well.

In our attempts to do this we need to remain vigilant for signs of disabling stress, which, as we well know by now, is counterproductive and which interferes with learning.

19

Work Through Strengths, By-pass Weaknesses

Education is a fine balance between addressing weakness and deficiency on the one hand, and broadening natural aptitude and interest on the other hand. We have tended to address the education of children by placing a lot of emphasis on addressing perceived weakness and deficiency. Hence our preoccupation with homework, special private tuition, remedial programmes, maths camps, and so on.

This approach to education is often called the 'deficit model'. It seeks to promote learning by focusing on deficiencies. When it is appropriate, this approach will lead to educational gains in a relatively short space of time. If this does not happen, there is nothing to be gained by persisting, other than the gradual erosion of the child's sense of self-esteem. These persistent learning deficits have been shown to be due to neuro-physiological underactivity, or even total lack of activity, in the parts of the brain which are active when unaffected people are studied doing the task in question.

In some situations, such as dyslexia, which is a specific learning disability for reading, a different approach to teaching may result in a separate and remote part of the brain becoming activated instead of the usual part of the brain called Wernicke's area, where word symbols are decoded to give meaning. This again illustrates the concept of brain plasticity, which is the ability of the brain to remodel itself to achieve function. However, the degree of reading fluency which is achieved when this happens is far less than in the 'normal' brain.

There are many areas of intellectual and academic development which may be deficient and for which there seems to be no chance of effective compensation. In these cases to persist in trying to produce learning is fruitless at best and harmful at worst. We are likely to end up with a young person whose self-esteem has been permanently diminished by repeated inability to meet our expectations.

We should have the courage to accept that some children will never succeed in some areas of the academic curriculum because their brains are not wired the right way. The sooner we discover this and adopt alternative strategies the sooner we can go about finding ways around the problem, and the sooner we can start supporting and enhancing the self-esteem of the young person involved.

To do this we abandon the deficit model and embrace learning based on natural strengths and aptitudes. The young person with ASD may have areas of intense interest which on the surface may appear to preclude learning 'general knowledge'. However, if we are creative we can turn this narrowness to our advantage by using the interest as a vehicle for adding learning. Let's look at a couple of hypothetical examples.

Henry is interested in international soccer scores. Let's say he knows that Brazil beat Argentina by 3 goals to 2 in their last game. What can he tell us about Brazil? Where is it? Who lives there? What is the weather like there? What grows there? Are there any ports there? What goods pass through the ports? Who makes the goods? What are they made of? Where do the raw materials come from? How do they get to the factory? What happens to it when the product is made? And so on. And what about Argentina?

Justine is fascinated by all the books written by Ewe Boremestiff. Where do the stories in these books take place? What can you tell me about these places? Who are the characters and what do they do? What are their homes like? Where do they buy their food? Where does the food come from? And so on.

You can become really good at finding questions about people's intensely narrow range of interests to help them extend their learning.

Try it.

20

Abandon the Standard Curriculum

I have heard it said that school teaches us how to pass exams, but not how to live an adult life. I will avoid the temptation to preach on this theme. Suffice it to say that for many young adults, including young adults with ASD, the standard curriculum, which is designed to provide a broad academic knowledge base, measured by exam results, is a danger to their intellectual and developmental health.

There is nothing intrinsically wrong with the standard curriculum, as far as it goes. It works for the majority of young people who attend our schools. However, there is a small group of young people for whom the standard curriculum is an irrelevance. This group of young people needs an education for life skills, not passing exams. And many of the people who fit into this group are young people with ASD.

The practical difficulty these young people face is that for understandable reasons of financial efficiency schools are organized to get people through the standard curriculum and through their exams. There is nothing left over for this small group who need an alternative. It would be nice if the person with ASD who is intensely interested in Mozart could spend more time in the music room, but there is no spare capacity for this. The schedule does not allow it.

It takes willingness and courage to depart from the straight and narrow in order to accommodate the person with ASD at secondary school. But in those schools that manage to do this the results for young people with ASD can be quite spectacular.

There is no fixed formula for how to do this. What is necessary is the willingness to apply the basic principles outlined in this book in whatever way seems to make sense at the time, and to be prepared to adjust things along the way as we learn what works well and what doesn't. You might make some mistakes here and there, but that is always better than if you had never tried to break out of the conventional mould.

It works best when this departure from the norm is planned, monitored and evaluated through the schools standard planning process. This involves the parents and young person (when age is appropriate for this), teachers directly involved with the young person and outside resource people such as an educational psychologist. Don't forget the importance of ensuring that the world experts on the person in question are given the role of 'Chair of the Board', at least to the degree of having speaking and voting rights at the table.

21

Teach Skills for Life

Steven Covey makes the point in his book *The 7 Habits of Highly Effective People* that it's always a good idea to begin with the end in mind.

We tend to take it for granted that we learn skills for life by some vague process of gradual assimilation over childhood that equips us for all the tasks that adults need to be good at – from managing a successful career as an independent member of society, to knowing how to manage personal finances, pay income tax, find a partner, bring up a family, pay the rent, stay in a relationship, feed the cat, keep the boss happy, water the plants, book the holidays, get the groceries, placate the neighbours…and so on and so on and so on.

There doesn't seem to be anything in the standard curriculum about this. I never had a class called 'Practical Skills for Getting on in Life'. If I had it would probably now be called 'Principles of Existential Behaviour' or some such fancy name.

I understand that what I knew as woodwork, metalwork, cooking, sewing, and all these practical subjects, are now called 'Technology'. Many of the young people I see need lots more of this than the curriculum allows them. But from what I see as an outside observer there is not much opportunity to take 'Tech' because we are all busy doing the other stuff the curriculum demands. I suppose this reflects a notion that a 'broad education' is good for all of us. What I know is that quite a lot of young people are turned off by this. But they would not be turned off if they could spend more time at school doing what they find interesting, hands-on and absorbing and can get jobs doing when they leave.

For the group of people we are discussing in this book, learning 'skills for life' is at least as important as, if not more important than, the standard curriculum. We have achieved nothing if these young people leave school not knowing how to start and maintain a conversation, or make a shopping list and then do the shopping in the local supermarket, or know about how to get and keep a job. The list goes on. Our challenge is to sort out how we are going to use our schools to deliver this 'skills for life' education.

Go figure.

22

Use Visual Approaches to Learning Whenever Possible

Always remember that the majority of people with ASD tend to think in pictures. A picture speaks a thousand words, so why waste your breath talking?

We have discussed this visual preference earlier, but it bears repeating that a whiteboard on the kitchen wall or the classroom wall with the week's timetable written up can say it all to a youngster with ASD. But don't ever forget – once it is on the whiteboard we are all committed to it. If we need to make a change this must be discussed and explained and then recorded on the board.

If there is a bit of the whiteboard that you can't plan for in advance, such as what are we going to do on Saturday afternoon, then at least put up some options.

We can use pictures to help with transitions or to help approach a new experience.

We can use photographs of our youngster doing something mundane, such as brushing his teeth, to act as a cue for this part of the morning routine. The more we can involve the person with ASD in devising and making a visual aid the more effective this is likely to be because he will have chosen something visual he thinks will work best, and he has invested his own energy and productivity into its making. In this way you will be putting into practice the principle of consulting the person himself for his knowledge of what is likely to work best for him.

23

Stay Concrete: Avoid Metaphor, Irony, Sarcasm, Cynicism, etc.

We use metaphor, simile and aphorism all the time. These add colour and emphasis to our conversation. A well-chosen metaphor can instantly convey a message that might take a good handful of words to paraphrase. Let's have some fun with this.

Ahah, the bad penny has turned up. What a sight for sore eyes. The worm has turned and here you are again lighting up my life. I thought you were being toffee nosed. But you came up smelling of roses. I could have climbed the wall when you didn't pull your socks up. You took me for a ride, you old son of a gun. Butter wouldn't melt in your mouth. You make me feel as high as a kite.

or

Hello. Good to see you. You look great. I am happy you are here. I thought you didn't like me very much. But you came. I was sad when I thought you weren't going to come. I was wrong, my friend. You do good things and I am pleased about this.

Sarcasm is another linguistic pitfall we can put in the path of our person with ASD. When we use sarcasm we make a statement in such a way as to imply that the opposite is what is intended. I deliberately make use of sarcasm in a later section of this part of the book when I end a description of an episode of uninformed mismanagement at school with the word 'Brilliant!'

Of course this is not at all brilliant, but I use the word sarcastically knowing that 97 out of 100 readers, on average, would know that I intend the opposite meaning, and hoping that my use of sarcasm reinforces the point I am making.

So, if you are not happy with what your person with ASD just did, make sure you are literal and not sarcastic.

As you become aware of the need to avoid figures of speech and stay concrete you will begin to understand the extent to which your everyday language is littered with these colourful expressions. You will begin to understand just how much of the verbal communication directed at the person with ASD is inherently confusing and unintelligible. He could begin to wonder how he could ever make sense of the world. These dawnings of new understanding come as stark reminders of just how much we have taken for granted in the past. Now you can begin to make a real difference.

24

Reinforce Teaching of Social Skills

I know a delightful young man of 17 who has Asperger syndrome. He agonizes over his inability to know how to start a conversation with a young woman he finds attractive. This reflects two interesting features of ASD: first, the ignorance of subtle nuances in social relationships, and second, the propensity to get 'stuck'.

One might find it difficult to help this young man. How does one teach somebody the fine art of dating? This is something that comes naturally to most of us, to varying degrees, but if we are asked to explain how it works most of us wouldn't have a clue — we just do it and get better at it by trial and error.

However, there is a real role for teaching young people with ASD some of the rudiments of effective interpersonal behaviour. We need to be sure that we remain concrete when we attempt this. Don't forget that people with ASD do not do stuff like manners, rudeness, intimacy, knowing when to speak and when to remain silent, knowing how long to maintain eye contact before it becomes threatening, knowing how to deal with a silence, knowing how to interpret the other person's facial expression...and so on.

On the other hand one often sees a younger person with ASD who has learnt to imitate the language and conversation of older people, usually adults, and who then talks this kind of mature language with anyone, anywhere, totally oblivious of the norms of behaviour which speak against talking with strangers, or in this case, talking *at* strangers. The problem here is that most people accosted in this way are somewhat charmed and disarmed by the apparent maturity of the young person. So the young person's approach is reinforced by the initial positive reaction he experiences. This positive feedback perversely encourages more of the same next time.

What is needed here is a distillation of the simpler rules of social etiquette. This is not the place for a discussion of this, other than to restate that social skills training can make a real difference for many young people with ASD.

John Elder Robison, a self-described 'Aspergian misfit' might help parents see their child in a different light. This is how John describes his isolation as a child:

> Many descriptions of autism and Asperger's describe people like me as 'not wanting contact with others,' or 'preferring to play alone.' I can't speak for other kids, but I'd like to be very clear about my own feelings: I did not ever want to be alone. And all those child psychologists who said 'John prefers to play by himself' were dead wrong. I played by myself because I was a failure at playing with others. I was alone as a result of my own limitations, and being alone was one of the bitterest disappointments of my young life.

He goes on to describe how he eventually gleaned some basic conversational rules (e.g. comment on the subject at hand, not on some completely unconnected topic that happened to be going through his head at the time), which made all the difference in his social development. Try googling him.

Just sharing the basic rules in a very concrete manner can be life changing. Sharing parts or all of this book with your child with ASD could also be a revelation. And it bears repeating that people with ASD can learn a great deal by reading 'social stories' specifically designed for their way of thinking. There are many available. An internet search will be rewarding.

25

Deal with Stress

We have already spent time discussing the problem that stress and anxiety pose for someone who has ASD and some of the techniques for self-help in relieving stress. If you need reminding you could revisit the relevant sections now or later.

In addition to the many practical techniques that can help the person with ASD deal with and minimize stress, it is important to know that many people with ASD respond well to medications designed to relieve anxiety and stress.

The most commonly used medications would probably be the SSRIs (selective serotonin re-uptake inhibitors), which increase the amount of naturally occurring free serotonin, a neurotransmitter, that lies between the cells of the brain. This increase in the levels of this neurotransmitter enhances useful connections between brain cells that can materially reduce the amount of stress and anxiety felt by the person who has ASD. This in turn allows clearer and more effective natural thinking to occur.

When an SSRI is started there is no immediately apparent beneficial effect. It takes up to four weeks for the maximum effect to develop, but changes can be noticed by the end of the first week of treatment. The SSRIs are convenient because they are taken only once a day and it doesn't particularly matter which time of the day this is, as long as it is roughly the same time each day. Taking the medication at breakfast seems to be convenient for most families.

A tiny proportion of young people can be sensitive to this class of medication. When this happens the result is a state of disinhibition that can resemble mania. This shows up as increased restlessness, excessive talking, increased emotional expression and loss of self-control.

It's best to start off with a small dose and gradually increase it if necessary.

Sometimes a more powerful medication can make the difference, but before we get to that stage we need to check that we have done everything we can to be sure all the other ingredients for success are being applied. We should always avoid the temptation to use medication instead of sound management strategies.

Your family doctor or paediatrician would be the best person to talk to about this, if she hasn't already made the suggestion.

26

Remember That Not Much Learning Occurs When There Is Stress

You should already know that confronting people with ASD while they are stressed out will not lead to learning. When you detect stress the best thing to do is to work with individuals to help them relieve their stress. Once they have calmed down and rebooted you can now now engage with them so as to help them learn whatever you would like them to know.

You will eventually come to recognize that there may be certain times in the day when it is best to think about learning. When you approach your role as parent or teacher remember to stay concrete. If you are solving an issue of behaviour, don't forget to get the young person to suggest solutions whenever this is appropriate. If you think the suggestion is not ideal, you can then ask whether there are any other possible solutions. Even though you may not shoot a hole in one (those metaphors!) you may come up with the right answer after two or three attempts.

After-school routines can be adjusted to acknowledge that the person with ASD arrives home stressed out. The thing they need first is food. You can even take it with you if you collect your child from school. Then we need a good chunk of time to chill out doing something relaxing, like playing on the computer. Only then are we ready to discuss what sort of day we had at school and begin our homework.

27

Remember That Punishment Does Not Produce Learning

Punishment is a technique used to reinforce the notion that logical consequences can modify behaviour. Logical consequences happen when you break the rules. Natural consequences happen when you run up against the forces of nature.

In general, punishment is a weak and ineffective tool compared to the power of consistently recognizing and rewarding good behaviours. However, despite its weakness, punishment is widely used in attempts to modify the behaviour of children and young people (and adults, of course).

When extended to persons with ASD punishment becomes an even more useless and pointless exercise, serving only to reveal that the person awarding the punishment has no understanding of ASD.

The problem is that the person with ASD who is being punished will inevitably have no understanding of the social codes and conventions whose norms he has just violated.

People with ASD just do not do 'codes' and 'conventions'. They are totally grounded in what appears to them to be obvious and logical. They can remember the basic rules a lot of the time, but when they are stressed they revert to their version of 'logical' behaviour. This usually involves telling it or doing it as they see it.

Thus, when the 13-year-old with ASD tells his maths teacher in class that he doesn't like her hairstyle he is merely stating the simple plain truth as he sees it. He is baffled when the teacher's response is to throw him out of the class for an audience with the headmaster, who then suspends him from school for three days. The young man remains baffled and still tells it as he sees it – he has learnt nothing except that sometimes adults behave unpredictably. He might also learn over time that to avoid a class all he needs to do is make a comment on the teacher's hair. Who is the dunce if this happens?

What is disturbing about this true scenario is that the maths teacher and the headmaster didn't figure out that by the age of seven or eight 'neuro-typical' children have already come to realize that discussing the teacher's hairstyle is not acceptable and that a comment on hairstyle would not occur to a normal 13-year-old who had chosen to be mischievous.

So we end up with a situation in which a 'punishment' produced no learning. The 13-year-old hasn't learnt anything useful. The maths teacher and the headmaster haven't learnt anything useful. And the boy's mother has uselessly lost three days' pay and had her job put at risk.

Brilliant!

(That's got sarcasm out of the way).

28

Avoid Power Struggles

The scenario about the 13-year-old in the previous section reflects the constant power struggle played out in secondary schools, where the power gradient uses sanctions in its effort to maintain what passes for social cohesion.

This is the time to refer to John Kenneth Galbraith's book called *The Anatomy of Power*. This is a pretty heavy read, but in essence he describes three types of power: coercive, conditional and condign.

- **Coercive power** is when I point a gun at you and tell you to give me your watch and wallet – bullying.

- **Conditional power** is when I offer you a one hundred dollar bill and you agree to provide a service – a day's gardening, perhaps – bribing.

- **Condign power** is the collective force that happens when I am a member of a democratic society which votes for its own government whose rules I agree to obey of my own free will – being responsible.

The problem with coercive power is that sooner or later a bigger and stronger bully comes along and turns the tables on the first bully. This makes coercive power inherently self-destructive over time. The cycle can repeat itself, of course, with one despot replacing another. Enlightenment might be a long time coming.

The problem with conditional power is that it lasts only as long as your ability to pay. Sooner or later you will probably go broke.

The beauty of condign power is that it is self-reinforcing, self-perpetuating and inherently indestructible. Its strength lies in its collective ownership.

I'll leave it to you to decide which of these three types of power is the most likely to succeed in the long run and which type tends to exist in schools. I'll leave it to you to decide which of these three options you would like young people to adopt as their personal philosophy. And I'll leave it to you to decide which of the three options you would vote for.

Now that you have voted how are you going to put your preference into practice in your interactions with the person with ASD? (Hint: this book provides lots of ideas on this – assuming, of course, that you voted for the third option – well, you did, didn't you?)

29

Specific Intervention Programmes That May Help

There are many specific intervention programmes offered for people with ASD, especially those at the severe end of the spectrum.

As far as I am aware the only specific behavioural intervention programme which has scientific evidence to show that it makes a positive difference is Applied Behavioural Analysis, often called ABA for short. The essence of ABA is that it requires you to analyse your child's behaviour so that you come to understand what the underlying motive is. Once you have a good idea what the reason for a particular behaviour is you are then in a better position to figure out what you need to change in order to help the child come up with something more useful. If you think back to the section in this book called 'Seek Alternative Explanations for Behaviour' you will see that there is no difference between that simple approach and ABA. It works.

There is one other behavioural intervention I would like to mention because my own research shows that this too can be effective in changing behaviour by reducing anxiety. This approach uses clinical hypnosis.

Clinical hypnosis is a process that allows a person to use a trance state to help his subconscious mind achieve beneficial changes in his own conscious thinking and behaviour. The role of the therapist is to help the person achieve a trance state and then make appropriate therapeutic suggestions. This is all under the control of the person in trance. It is a mistake to think of hypnosis as something somebody 'does' to somebody else. The person enjoying trance remains in complete control of their own thinking and actions before, during and after trance.

Clinical hypnosis can be used as a general tool to promote regular relaxation and feelings of comfort and balance. This is helpful for older children and adults with ASD who experience general non-specific anxiety.

Clinical hypnosis can also be used to deal with a specific cause of distress, if there is one. Some examples include verbal bullying by classmates, school avoidance due to particular aspects of the school (such as a particular teacher who makes the child feel frightened) and reluctance to swim in a local lake with other classmates.

Clinical hypnosis for specific issues like these entails a process called guided imagery in which, in trance, a mental image of a desired outcome is induced and then intensified. This process of mental imagery under trance is effective in allowing the child to change specific aspects of brain function so that the person is able to feel differently about specific things that they would like to change.

In younger children, who, by nature of being young children, are very good at going in and out of awake trance states all by themselves, this guided imagery works without the induction of a formal trance which would be needed for older children and adults. If you remind yourself about how expert children with ASD are at daydreaming you already know, but probably didn't realize it, that these same children are really good at going into a trance because, after all, there is no difference between a daydream and a trance. It takes only a couple of minutes to help the child sort out whatever is bothering him using awake hypnosis.

Think about it!

30

Specific Intervention Programmes That Have No Proof That They Work

Novel educational programmes

There are many educational programmes proposed by eminent authorities which claim to make a specific beneficial difference for a child with ASD. The fact that there are so many of them probably reflects the fact that no single one is superior to any of the others. After all, there are lots of 'remedies' for the common cold because none of them work – if there was one that did work it would instantly become the market leader and the rest would fall by the wayside.

Just ponder. If you treat the common cold with a medication from the pharmacy it will last for two weeks. If you use a home-remedy handed down from your grandmother it will last for 14 days. If you don't use any treatment at all it will last for a fortnight. It doesn't matter what you do. The cold will be gone in the same time period. You would be fooling yourself if you thought that your treatment made a difference to the course of the disease.

If you think about educational programmes in the same way as you think about remedies for the common cold you might pause for a bit more thought.

It's possible and indeed probable that none of them offer any advantage over what a family working with their local school and local special education services can achieve. Proponents and consumers of this type of programme always claim that they provide additional benefit, but then they would wouldn't they? Things are inevitably going to improve. It is so easy to conclude that it is something special that you did that has led to this improvement.

So I don't know how much added benefit, if any, these special programmes give the child. I don't think anybody else does either. What I do know is that there is always the possibility that a large transfer of wealth from the family to a private provider will take place to the advantage of the provider and the disadvantage of the family, who may well be left only with shattered dreams and huge debts.

Here are some of the educational approaches I know of. This is by no means an exhaustive list.

- Treatment and Education of Autistic and Communication-Handicapped Children (TEACCH)
- facilitated communication
- discrete trial training
- auditory integration training
- sensory integration therapy.

In my local community none of the children with ASD I know receive special programming beyond what is planned and delivered for them in their own local school paid for by the government education budget. I don't need to harp on about the benefits of belonging to and living within your own local community and using local community resources. The approaches I advocate in this book, when adopted by local communities as small as a single classroom or as large as a local village or suburb can be hugely powerful in making that special difference for the person with ASD.

Don't let feelings of desperation or guilt or shortcoming blind you to the need to make a careful evaluation of what you spend your money on and what alternative opportunities you are giving away in the process. It's always possible that a good holiday will do more for you and your family than 'treatment'.

Specific medical and 'scientific' programmes

I can state categorically that there is no valid scientific evidence that any single medical or physiological or other type of treatment intervention has ever been proved to 'cure' autism spectrum disorder. There are many of these 'nostrums' lying in wait for the unwary family.

In spite of the absence of reliable scientific proof of efficacy and effectiveness many families spend huge amounts of money and run up crippling debts in order to pay for these nostrums. Some even go public to raise funds, which in turn creates widespread misinformation along the lines that ASD can be 'cured'. This is a cruel deception.

Some of the more widely touted medical interventions which remain either totally unproven or have actually been scientifically shown to be useless include

- dietary modification, such as gluten free or casein (dairy) free diets

- digestive enzyme supplementation
- free fatty acid (omega 3) supplementation
- secretin treatment
- hair analysis
- chelation therapy
- hyperbaric oxygen therapy
- stem cell therapy (injecting cells harvested from unborn rabbits, for example!).

I can also state categorically that there is no valid scientific evidence that any single medical or physiological or other type of treatment intervention has ever been proved to 'cause' autism spectrum disorder. Specifically it is important to emphasize here that MMR (measles, mumps and rubella) immunisation given at 15 months of age has now been conclusively proven to have no role whatsoever as a cause of ASD. The research that claimed this has been totally discredited and the doctors who made the claim have been struck off. Their research has been labelled fraud and the research paper in which the claims were first made has been withdrawn by the prestigious medical journal that published it.

I have been around long enough to have personally witnessed the devastating consequences of measles in young children, and rubella infections in newborn babies. We will never know how many preventable consequences of these illnesses occurred in people who did not receive MMR because of this fraud. I'm sorry to end this section on such a dismal note, but this is stuff that can seriously ruin people's lives.

**REMEMBER
THE ONLY BEHAVIOUR YOU CAN
CHANGE IS YOUR OWN**

These are my final words.
No further comment needed.
Thank you for getting this far and Good Luck!